Shades of Ebony
Epigrams of My Life

Jonathan W. Fields

To order additional copies of this book, contact:
Xlibris
1-888-795-4274
www.Xlibris.com
Orders@Xlibris.com

DEDICATION

I dedicate this book to my parents, John and Nellie Fields, who worked hard and sacrificed much, so I could be a success in life. Their undying love and support provided a beacon of guidance through many difficult times. Without John and Nellie my accomplishments would be non-existent.

My Love, Your Love, Our Love!

Introduction

As a 60's child growing up in New York City, during the height of the Civil Rights Movement, I found adolescence both frightening and exciting.

I remember eating mayonnaise sandwiches, watching I Spy, on black and white television, and ingesting "Dick and Jane" schoolbooks. I aliso reflect on a latch key life as an only child. No time for fun! Fast maturation was a must then. Can't be a kid, there's too much responsibility to learn. What a strange paradox, I can be both the man-of-the-house and the only child, simultaneously. Where's Dr. Alvin Poussaint when you need him?

Hard working, two job parents rounded out my household. It was their example that laid the foundation for my future. But it was the New York backdrop and a vivid imagination that filled the void of an introspective mind.

I remember blackouts, garbage strikes, the 68 civil rights riots, teacher's strikes, the slaying of John F. Kennedy, Martin Luther King Jr., Bobby Kennedy and Malcolm X. The deaths of Jimi Hendrix, Janis Joplin, Sammy Davis, Jr., Jim Morrison, Adam Clayton Powell, Sharon Tate, Rock Hudson, John Wayne, Louis Armstrong and Babe Ruth. I remember

the New York Knicks, Jets, Nets and even the N. Y. Bets. My love for basketball began with, Dr. "J", Willis Reed, Sonny Dove, Tiny Archibald, Clyde Frazier, Earl 'The Pearl' Monroe, Phil Jackson, Red Holzman, Billy Paultz, Jessie Dark, Harthorn Wingo, John Roche, Herman Helicopter, The Master Cylinder, Jackie Jackson and Earl Manigault. I remember listening to WWRL, WBLS, WABC, Hank Spann, Frankie Crocker, Ken 'Spider' Webb, Ken Anderson, Jazzy Joyce, Herbie 'The Love Bug', Kid Capri, Taki 183, Kurtis Blow, Sir Monti Rock III, Blue Magic, Black Ivory, Terry Tuff, Ronnie Dyson, The Spinners, The Unifics, Sugar Hill Gang, Kool Herc, Mellie Mell and Grand Master Flash. Partying at the Cave, The Tunnel, Lauiticuis, Fantasy Island, Studio 54, Boston Road Ballroom, Lloyd Price turntable and various Brooklyn house parties.

Who can forget Earth day, Woodstock, Walkin' on the moon, the Vietnam War, the Cold War, the war on crime, Jimmy Carter, Richard Nixon, Ronald Regan, Abe Beame, John Lindsey and Mayor Koch.

Television brought excitement every night with Batman and Robin, Johnny Carson, The Brady Bunch, The Flying Nun, The Late, Late Show, The

Mod Squad, Thriller Theater, The Million Dollar Movie, Six Million Dollar Man, The Avengers, The Green Hornet, The Jefferson's, Good Times, Sanford and Son, Days of Our Lives, General Hospital and Another World. I survived the AIDS epidemic, legionnaires disease, Ebola virus, crack wars, gang violence, the rise and fall of heroin, marijuana, boat, PCP, glue, meth, rush, micro dot, orange sunshine and cocaine.

My formal education remembers PS132, PS82, Sacred Heart Middle and High School, Queens Prep, Roosevelt High, Taft High, Elizabeth Seton College, The Bronx Community College, Benedict College, The University of South Carolina, North Carolina Central University, Howard University and Pacific Western University.

My employment memories abound with S. C. State Hospital, Veterans Hospital, Harambee Treatment Center, Taylor Manor Hospital, Maryland Dept. of Corrections, Carroll County General Hospital and Vanguard Services to name just a few.

I enjoyed living and growing up literally around the world via schools and military life. I've lived in Barstow, Ca., Corpus Christi, TX., Millington, Tenn., Great Lakes, Ill., San Diego, Ca., Oakland, Ca., San Bernardino, Ca., Raleigh, N. C., Columbia, S. C., Durham, N. C., Chicago, Ill., Boston, Ma., Andover, Ma., Subic Bay, Republic of the Philippines, K-Bay, Hawaii, Okinawa and Iwakuni, Japan, Guam, Korea and Bangkok, Vietnam.

These images fed my desire to dream. Those dreams later manifested themselves into interludes of poetic contradictions and illustrations, i.e. my interpretations of life, death and taxes.

This book takes both experience and didactic material and weaves a colorful and detailed tapestry into my personal insights and perspectives. At times it's both abstract and autobiographical in its presentation. However the exposing of ones idiolect through poetic justice can be difficult at best. To define my forty five years of living as "just poetry" would be like simplifying the message, diminishing the truth, belittling the sweat, minimizing beauty, ignoring death, and underestimating the power of love.

Thanks for allowing me to share my interludes with all who love and feel humanities vibes.

Table of Contents

AN ANGELS HORROR

Hate breeds evil
By the storm encased night.

Black clouds of hell
Darken heaven born skies.

Bringing much sorrow
And tears to an angel's eye.

Putting quite a wound
In his much cherished heart.

But he bleeds not with blood,
But with empathy.

AN ODE TO A CONVICT

The echoes reflect voices of fear,
Voices of shame, voices of hate.

Time spent reminiscing about convoluted justice.
Nappy headed images of my manifest destiny.

I eat food with preservatives,
I bathe in water treated with chemicals.

My cell illuminates with the aura of the foreboding.
I am a destitute prisoner.
My crime is irrelevant,

My time nebulas.

15 to 20 for stupid choices,
5 to 10 for the quick easy bucks,
7 to 10 for addictions unknown!

But 30 to life,
Oh my God!
The ultimate in Hammurabi's code.
My life for your life.

Individual stupidity for neo-governmental slavery…
The ultimate eye-for-an-eyeism!

Truly a society confused!
Lock me down and others more vile will replace me.

Evolution makes me indestructible!
Look at the statistics.
Lock up 10, 110 take my place,
Execute 30, 330 more homicides are late night news.

Evolution's made me immortal,
Mankind labels me scandalous,
But the media colors me glamorous.

I am like cockroaches,
I resist execution,
I surmount extermination!
I transcend conventional genocide.

My numbers are growing America!
Cockroaches are criminals.
Criminals are cockroaches.
I am here to stay America.

The Underground Railroad…extinct.
The Civil Rights Movement—-extinct.
The Black Panthers…extinct.

Cockroaches…are here to stay.
Criminals…are here to stay.
Except it America,
I am you worst nightmare…and I am growing.

Keep building more prisons America,
I need a place to stay.

Upgrade your jails President Bush,
I need to expand my operations.

You feed me, you house me, you fear me,
But you'll never stop me!

I am here to stay America!
Criminals never die, they just multiply!

AURA OF DEPRESSION

A troubled soul adrift in pain,
Searching for a relief not yet available.

No substitute for experience can be found.
No shortcut to success is in sight.

Can I skip my lessons learned?
Through blood, sweat and tears?

Must I hurt more today than yesterday?
So much pain for so little pleasure.

My God, my Savior!
Why have you forsaken my pain?

I pray for redemption,
Yet fail repeatedly.

I love hard and crash even harder.
Few give as much as this twice battered soul.

Fewer still have risen from the ashes of despair like me.
Do I get a metal of honor for 45 years of survival?

My life seems so worthless,
So much of a waste.

But Dr. Suicide and me
Refuse to bond.

I've lost my dignity, respect and pride.
However, I am not ready to surrender!
I refuse to quit!

My Boo believes in me, loves me pushes me.
Her support energizes me!
I'll continue to fight!

It's all up to me to weaken the storm.
A silver lining lies miles ahead.

My focus is adjusted, my goals are in sight.
There's a chance I'll be back, better than ever.

No more pain, no more pressure,
Free from despair.

I have to believe this,
I must believe this.

My soul depends on me to believe this!
I must! I will! I do!

BASKETBALL ON GUAM

9

It's a sunny day about ninety-five
I'm trying to keep my spirits alive.
The humidity's a bitch and I can't sweat.
Me and gator aid's a sure bet.

A game's on the tube and that's right on,
However Detroit just sang their Swan song.
Atlanta got beat three games to one,
I am sure Dominique Wilkins just had fun.

One more quarter is all I can stand,
Dr. "J" the superstar lost his man.
I look at the pros to inspire my run,
That's when it really comes down to fun.

Off to the gravel for war this day.
I wonder who's brave enough to come this way?
I'll shoot a jumper just to warm up,
As tried and true as coffee in my cup.

My turn-a-rounds nasty, that's no lie.
If you root for Ralph Sampson it's in your eye.
I'll drive to the hoop to keep them honest,
Unless you play pro ball it ain't enough polish.

Out over the field who's that I see?
Why it's five hospital corpsmen pretending to be.
They dress up like ball players out for a game,
To risk pride playing me, it's a damn shame.

Milton, Mark, Glen and a jock named Ernie,
The way they play, what me worry?
Cyrus has also ventured this way!
I love it when scrubs make my day!

The first to fold is big bad Mark,
Being seven-foot-five made him tallest in the park.
He was very little challenge to my foot speed.
Fifteen to two, please excuse my greed.

Next is Glen Edwards from NYC.
Only a fool from there would dare play me,
Ten jumpers, five hooks and that's it man.
Don't ever bother to shake my hand.

What's this? Who dares? It's Mr. Boast.
Boy what an easy game for me to host.
He's big and strong that's no lie,
But he's easy to fake, so see ya'…bye!

What kind of drugs are they serving at lunch today?
They have to be good for Cyrus to play.

I'll increase my range to forty-four feet,
What else is there to do when his "D" is so weak?

Now I've had my snacks I need a real meal,
Send me high jumping Milton I need a few steals.
He has a good jumper and can even dunk,
But his game is soft, hell dance to my funk.

He takes and early lead, I worry very little,
Coming from behind's like playing a fiddle.
Two blocks, one steal, I am now in command,
It's four games to none, I control this land.

We play for the fifth to have bragging rites,
By now it's dark, someone turn on the lights.
My bank shot is true, jumpers on the mark.
Hey Milton! You're being blown out of the park!

I've won all five with barely a sweat,
They all leave disappointed, that's what you get.
I am the king of the pass, block and slam.
I guess that's why they had to scram.

They call me "Big Moses" and I can tell no lie,
I love the name, 'cause I am That Kind of Guy,
But if you dare play me, you best be ready,
Or you'll just wind up like J. Paul Getty.

Since the moon is out and I now stand-alone.
It seems it's best I just go home,
For another day is over and the King I'll stay
To live and be Moses another day.

BLUE COLLAR WORKER

In a world I never made,
I am an insect.

My existence is mandated
By powers beyond my control.

I exist to eat, I exist to breed,
I am an insect.

To survive I must pass my genes to my progeny.
I need other insects to evolve.

There are forces out there that seek to exterminate me.
I must develop immunity to their poisons.

I must fight through sheer force and numbers.
Destroy some of us, but miss most of us.

We will survive because we are insects.
Death be not proud.

Century's before we fought.
Millenniums later we fight.

I am an insect.
I will survive!
I must survive....
Lest I be crushed!

BOOM! BOOM! BOOM!

The explosions are all around us now,
Shall we run to take cover?
Or shall we continue to fight the unknown?

I can feel the hot breath of bombs against my brow,
Once more the stench of burnt flesh sickens me.

High technology against flesh and bone?
What chance do I have against the bomb?

My forty-five is a good weapon for the programmed fool,
But how do I halt a Sherman Tank?

Who's my back up against the F-14's that fly overhead?
If I am trained to preserve life, why am I damning it?

I run for a shelter that doesn't exist,
Don't they know we're not expected to survive this kind of war?

It's who pushes the button first!
The roars of bombs are closer now,
Almost to my flank!

We started out fifty, now it's just me,
But where shall I hide?
Here or there?

Rubble around me, death almost on top of me,
What shall I do?
Maybe a prayer will help?

My back is uncovered, my cover lost,
My flag is torn and scorched.

I am trying to keep my sense of liberty,
Love of home, freedom and democracy.

Where's my Commander?
Who's in charge here?
I was given a rifle with training obsolete.

I was left for dead, but told to fight on…
Another bomb, one less hiding place.

It's just you and me now,
Sickle against the flag.

I don't know you from Adam, but kill you I must.
You know me even less, but death's in your eyes too.
It's man verses man, the age-old plight,
We fight more for principle than for a meal.

Not long ago our cause was freedom, belief in our land.
Two left on earth, not giving an inch.

What cause do we fight for now?
There's no one left to award the winner.

My towns in rubble, laid waste by the bomb,
Your land is worse, we pushed the button first.

If there's a good reason for why we fight
Please tell me now, because I need to know.

Your weapon is loaded and so is mine,
Who-so-ever lives through this ordeal is truly King.

A man with a new world, though laid to waste
You'll rule unobstructed in a juryless court.

No matter what happens, I can't pull the trigger, so you win by default.

My principles are strong and to the point,
I believe in life and caring for the sick.

You're just a war machine, a believer in strife
While I am a Hospital Corpsman, a preserver of life.

CHOCOLATE "BOO" FUDGE

1 Cup Honey
1 Cup Brown Sugar
2 Lbs. Love
4 Lbs. Jonathan
3 Lbs. Boo
1 Tsp. Sugar
1 Cup Chopped Nuts
2/3 Cup Undiluted Breast Milk

Combine Jonathan, brown sugar, his Boo
And honey in a king-sized bed.
Bring together each other kissing constantly.
Continue kissing and feeling each other vigorously,
For 20 to 30 minutes,
Between silk sheets.

Mix their love until well blended
And say the magic words to each other…
I Love You.

Hold each other for 22 seconds.
Remove from heat.
Cool at room temperature.

Makes approximately 365 lbs, or days of Chocolate "Boo" Fudge.

DEATHS CONTRACT

I come and go, here and there,
When I come, when I strike,
Even I know not where.

Because I am no color, no form, no shape,
It's hard to spot me at the gate.

I feel the need as quick as a flash,
And when I hit, it's eternal whiplash.

When I appear, I just stop, and wait.
No preparation exists for such a fate.

So when I strike please bare me no malice,
There's only one ticket to that great black palace.

I am not even prejudice, in who I smite,
He may be black, yellow, green or white.

Be it the sunniest day, or the darkest night.
You might be at work or watching a heavyweight fight.

I'm doing you and injustice you might rightly say,
But it's really a favor in a strange way.

With all the poverty, prejudice and crime I see,
My justice is swift, my lessons the key!

If your trade includes rape, murder or even theft,
There's only one answer…Signed Mr. Death!

DON'T DIS' MY HEART

My heart holds words that can't be spoken.
It cherishes vivid memories of happiness, ecstasy and joy,
But lets hurt slip through it like a sieve.

Although porous and elastic, it has its limits…
Tiny fissures arise when it's filled with deceit and lies.

Tearful moments pierce it's delicate exterior,
As tense moments pass slowly by,
Leaving it vulnerable to the infections of despair.

Yes, there is room enough for you to walk around
In every corner of this heart if you choose.
But the pace will only satisfy the heart that is true.

A heart that knows no bounds, to the human need,
To love and to be loved.

FREEDOM

Freedom is not yet apparent
We know very little Freedom

To be Free is what you need to see,
Therefore we're blind.

To some Freedom is MD 20/20, others call Freedom crack

I call this the inability to see beyond ones nose

Conversely, what I call Freedom may be strange to some

Freedom to me is expression, via pencil and pen

GOODBYE

You gave me death as an ultimate gift,
I thought it was love, but no not this!

I shamed my wife, family and child,
Being totally irresponsible, stupid and wild.

If death be my reward for a shameful act,
I am one knee down, please take it back!

It's too, too late, I've paid my price,
Risky unprotected sex in exchange for my life.

As I write this will I hope someone will bereave,
Death by stupidity this legacy will read.

HONEST LIFE

My emotions scream with pain,
A heart beset with scars.

Betrayal of the soul,
No trust or comfort in union.

Death be a permanent escape,
But why flee from courage,
To face a deadly foe?

To conquer the spell of deceit,
That is a thirst to be satisfied.

A weakness is a demon to be surmounted,

But to win,
Oh the joy to win!

I feel liberated, to wrest the
Yoke of confusion from my bosom.

To have purpose,
To feel trustworthy,
To be happy.

These are the rewards of life,
To live one must have worth.

To follow the song's of the soul,
One must live.

But to be,
One must give all, honestly.

HONESTY

Truth is a feeling for a better tomorrow

Truth means you'll never deceive your brother

Truth denotes honesty and wholeness

Truth cleans the soul of the devils residue

Truth allows self-assuredness

It beams the light of confidence and trust

I REMEMBER 1980

I remember 1980
A year of disillusion
A year of loneliness
A year of disbelief

I remember losing a job,
A wife, a friend, a son and my self-respect,
All in one fell swoop!

I remember confrontations in Popeye's Chicken,
High speed chases on Assembly Street.

I begged when substance was but an illusion.
I cried when child and father were split.
Relationships became wars, homes battlefields,
And bedrooms DMZ's.

Only a fool would cross his wife's DMZ.
My insecurities became her target.
A mans short comings fueled a wife's dissolution.

I lost confidence in myself, I forgot who I was.
I had no purpose!

I became a beast who survived for the moment.
Responsibility? Why bother,
I am paying my dues!
After midnight all bill collectors sleep.
Don't they?

Perhaps my roommate will cut me some slack,
A new job might renew my self-esteem,
At least that's the hope.
He wants half the rent...yesterday!
No money, no lodging, no lodging, no respect.

An aura once positive, once electric,
Is now rocky and dimming.
A man once full of potential and promise,
Now walks alone.

Is this the American way?
Why can't I bounce back?
Walk into the sunset smiling?
Just another pipe dream
Waiting to be shut down...huh!

I remember it being difficult for me to see white,
But live black,
To wish for prosperity,
But languishing in poverty.

I long for happiness,
But constantly battle sorrow.

An inability to focus,
My dreams shattered.

I remember when my only possession was a basketball.
A poor image of a father,
Even less as a man.
Who wants to be bothered with a rusted tin can?

Who accepts my shortcoming?
Why build when a foundations weak?
Will you love me after I am eulogized?
Speak and then be the voice of clarity.

Lead me to the fountain of confidence,
Let me drink the sweet nectar of awareness.
Baptize me in fluids of redemption.
A predisposition for failure? Not!

Sometimes I miss the ex-wife, the in-laws, the drama.
It seems without domestic strife no man is whole.
But why must I be like "the horse with no name?"
How can I fight fair, if I am sucker punched by my past?

In truth there's no one answer.
A man must do what his fate requires.
With a strong will to survive
My most difficult battles are eventually won.

But still, I query myself about that year.
Was I in the wrong time?
Or was I in the right time
With the wrong purpose?

Some day these questions will be word.
For fate to complete my saga.
My quest must mirror my purpose.
Then the healing can begin.
The closure is real.
I remember.

Take the time to explore

Touch me and my soul

Feel me, let your essence and mine entwine

Don't resist me, resistance is benign

Love me, call me as you would yourself

Break the film, all that is between us is doubt.

I Want You!!

Please be me

Now neither you nor I exist

The Almighty has forged a new Nebula

NOW WE'RE US!

I WON

I lost a battle with myself today
A fight that made me a beginning

I lost a war by a hundred to one
And now I'm truly a winner.

I fell short by a scant margin
A hair's breath to be precise.

But you know I can't say I am very upset,
'Cause I lost and that means I won!

I WANT YOU

KIM

Essence of young womanhood

Sister girl and saint

A voice of respect

Honor thy anger

Pay homage to her beauty

Erect is her attitude

No deceit can bedazzle you

The truth is your foundation

Strong is your morality

A sprinkle of naivety

A dash of creative experience

Leader by birthright

Non-conformist till death

Woman you be,

Lady you'll stay,

Girl you evolved from,

Your legacy lies in your strength,

The sum total of ebony parts,

Continue to strive.

Conquer the untruth

KNOWING

Because my mind remembers you,
It does not fantasize of who you are.

Because I imagine others want to know you as I do,
I cannot imagine that I will feel this way again.

Because I want to be where you are,
Not dictate where you go.

Because I want to share you,
Not keep you for myself.
Because I want to change nothing of you,
But willfully watch you grow.

Because I rejoice in your happiness,
I do not conspire to steal it.

Knowing the kind of woman you are,
I flourish in your care.

Because of knowing you,
I no longer wonder…if I am in Love.

LESSER CREATURES

Man must be reckoned with,
The decree has been made.

Only the once lesser creatures
Need dominance over a world we never made.

Man never deserved to rule.

Pollution and sludge must not
Continue to blemish our environment.

The scars of apathy must not further insult our realm.

Thus the wee creatures of the earth must unite,
And not barter but control.

His trice ignorant reign must cease.

LOVE SPIDER

Here I am,
I know you're there!

I see you!
You're waiting to snare me.

Please capture me.
Please devour me.

I am a lonely fruit fly,
And you're Love Spider!

I am entwined in you web
Awaiting your pursuit.

Please Love Spider sink your fangs in me,
Share my life juices.

I want to be part of you,
In you Love Spider.

I'll not struggle, here I'll stay,
But not long.

Thank you, Love Spider,
THANK YOU!

MADE TO ORDER LOVE

In the year 2000 you won't have to barter,
You'll have made to order love.
It won't matter who your brother is,
Because instead of war you'll have love.
Nobodies worn out dreams,
Just instant good old-fashioned fun.

Porn won't mean much to you,
Because everything is free.
You'll have too much body
And very little mind,
Because of made to order love.

Special outlets will be designed for degrees of sex
From mild to outlandish.
With the introduction of sex stamps
Even the poor won't have to do without.
All of this possible,
With made to order love.

My friend, love will be totally free,
And so will the experienced lover.
Random lust and social sex will abound.
It matters not
That emotion will be deleted from your mind at birth.

Worry not my friend,
Because childbirth as you knew it
Will disappear altogether.
You'll have to qualify with the state
For "creation papers" with one chance
Out of thirty to be approved.

It seems cruel but the price is small…pleasure for freedom.
You see the population is the trend of the past
And pleasure is now.

In this world,
War is a memory and freedom a dream.
Everyone's a lover
And no nation dominates our globe.

The world's new covenant has long since replaced our outdated governments.
They say, ten births per year are all we need to survive.
But who's to say you're going to be part of that ten?
They say no guarantees granted.

Remember the lust of the 60's, 70's, 80's and 90's?
The made to order love of the now era transcends that.
Please don't recall the joy and happiness of freedom,
Nor the benevolence of birth.

It's not considered normal to think of such foolishness.
If this is not genocide

Then what of the future
Of man as a species?

I remember stories by my
Great-great-great-grandmother
Speaking of joy, ecstasy, passion and pain.
She spoke of the joy of children.
The experience of freedom…What's that grandmother?

She said status was based more on your income than your law.
Isn't it a pity that we who dominate the cities
Must ourselves be ruled by a federal warlord?
Who other that God should control a natural law?

When will we realize that we are destroying ourselves slowly?
I guess it has something to do with
"The new trend"…social suicide.

The irony of all this is the ruler of the earth, wind and atom is
In turn ruled by a machine!
The ultimate computer incapable of giving birth,
Feeling pain, comprehending pleasure or peering into
The eyes of a lovers stare.

But it does understand one thing,
Giving the world it's one true great gift
It gave us made to order love!

MEMORIES

Memories are really bad,
Trying to relive that which you never had.

As I listen to "Freak of the Week"
My recall ability begins to peak.

But my God! I think, what's it all about?
Right now a voice, just a little above a shout.

It's in the past, lay buried forever more,
A long time ago, too long to be sure.

But why recall only that which makes you sad?
When as people we should strive to be ever glad.

I muse the past from time to time,
It's just a bothersome act of mine.

Sometimes I feel really high,
Until I remember the ultimate why.

Reflection is fine when kept in check,
When it runs amok, it's time to forget.

Keep pushing forward, climb one more rung,
Lest your mind become useless for days to come.

MR. RAINDROP

I challenged a raindrop today,
Drop do you dare come out to play?

He fell to earth from parts unknown,
A curious fellow shaped like a cone.

He danced and frolicked like an animate fool,
A heart full of fun, a manner most cool.

Off my nose and to my chin,
Should I swallow my Buddy or bust a grin?

No words asunder from a liquid prism,
Be this a form of wisdom?

But alas his life cycle must come to an end,
A short goodbye to a seasonal friend.

He descends to a more hostile abyss,

His cool damp nature I'll surely miss.

Only his ghost whisking by,
Guarantee's his return from a tomb less sky.

Tomorrow I'll awake so full of glee,
Cause a challenge will ring forth once more from me.

And a raindrop will answer it just watch, you'll see.

MY BOO

Don't reject non-traditional romance or unborn love.

Don't turn your back to misunderstandings, images or unsaid actions.
Forget hurts past or unreasonable foreboding,
Try to feel as I do and try to form a bond.
Believe with your heart, not with you scars.

I feel the need for love, not just a physical embrace.

I want you because it's written that way, not because you exist.

A vulnerable heart and an objective mind are all I have to offer.
Can you accept me as I am, the way I do you?
Or am I another romantic junkie on the way to another high?
Do you feel the fork in the road?
Will it make us whole?
I truly feel that you could love me as I love you,
To challenge the world and strive for goals.

But friendship and love can't survive
unless they respect each other.

Will you be my friend until the end of
time, and maybe even my lover?

When times are bad will you be my
friend and tell the truth?

Don't feed my ego or agree with me just
to make amends.
Be honest with me and if it's called for,
be blunt.

I'll be there to help you when you're
down, no matter what the cost.

Because not even death can divide a bond as strong as time.
Not even Satan can harm a friend.
We're strong now, but growth will give us greater strength.
Love me as my dreams love you.

Let's fall in love Boo, let's fall in love.

MY SON

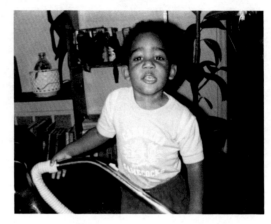

My life's essence is transformed to Jonathan
His mannerisms are copyright.

His little hands mimic Daddy's toil.
Black Power via Black Love.

A wee being with the weight of the world,
His future, on his bitty shoulders.

My mind is his reference,
My muscles, his protection.

Love illustrates our true bond.
Touch me Jonathan and transfer auras between us.

My essence is your legacy.

Continue to bond, yours is the beginning.
My life must approach its prime.

My existence fears it's own limitations,
But our love is endless.
You are My Son.

NEW LIFE

I see a light
A light I see
And it apparently
Belongs to me.

This light brings freedom
To a once enslaved man
I the northern native to
This southern land.

I've always noted
In times of strife
That I would soon be
Released to a better life.

So now is my time
To go from trot to run
To bask in a new
Creative sun.

Let no prejudice stop me,
Lest I retard myself.
Only my creative freedom
Will bring true intellectual wealth.

OUR NATURAL FOE

It's called mistletoe, why I don't know?
But I tell you this, it's got to go!

People claim it's a charm,
That's what I hear,
A sign of happiness, kissing and cheer.

I think it's sad, actually sickening to me!
'Cause in the wild, it's a sight to see.

This plants a parasite, that's right, it's so!
Oaks and Pines say this, and they should know!

So if you cherish this plant, go right ahead,
But me, a Weeping Willow, I'd rather be DEAD!

PLANTS

A potted green wonderment stands forever tall
To grow, to blossom, to even smell sweet.
I love my green friends,
They require only my concern.

See how they reach for that, which we take for granted,
They thrive on the positives of nature,
The water, air, earth and wastes of others.
A blossom opens revealing a hidden jewel.

Seeds for another life just waiting to be born,
Gee they smell nice, oh what a fragrance.
Colors that brighten and bring good cheer.
I love my pretty plants all strong and tall.

Now the humble honeybee, he knows what a good friend
These green allies are,
He appreciates their golden nectar,
He loves their outgoing personality.

Drink deep, they seem to say to him.
He sips and enjoys the liquid of life,
In return he pays for the privilege in pollination,
For a friendly drink, this seems fair.

Oh what buddy's we seem to be,
My plants, the honeybee and me.
But who's this that enters the fray?
Why it's Mr. Crab Spider, now what does he want?

He does not drink "brew" so why is he here?
The honeybee's not amused by this dangerous guest,
My plant also feels the omen of death.
Spiders are disliked by plant and bee alike.

Is he here to make trouble on this stage of calm?
His movements are queer as he turns left then right,
Can it be that his diet will change on this special day?
From meat to vegetable is too much to hope for.

My fern appears nervous at the spider's presence,
I don't blame him for I would be too,
But the honeybee is unmoved and I don't know why,
It's his life that's in danger not you, not I.

A yellow green zip is all we see
My friend has disappeared just that fast,
Why didn't he say goodbye?
I thought we had an understanding.

I even thought we were friends.
My Snake Plant weeps because he's lost another,
The bright green leaves have somehow turned blue.

Tears of dew have fallen from my Buddy's surface.

I guess we both know what happened.
My Honeybee was sacrificed so life can go on.
Which in turn helps my tulips.
But why Mr. Honeybee?

We weep together this night,
My plants and I,
And even though we know there was a murder
We excuse the crime.

Tomorrow morning will bring warm dew,
A clear day, full of sweetness and calm,
Another blossom will open to reach and kiss the sun
Another Honeybee has already replaced his brother.

He too will drink and make us happy,
For his task will be unchanged
His life mimics his predecessor
My plants love Mr. Honeybee, my plants love life,
And I love my plants.

POET'S PROMISE

I see the home of winter,
The home of spring,
The green leaves of summer,
What will autumn bring?

The rolling mountains,
And rock hillsides.
Many painters have seen
What a cloudy day hides.

It's not just a robin,
But an olive green frog,
No contrast whatsoever
To an old man's dog.

What the earthworm did,
I touch and fear,
But the raven in flight
I can only peer.

The cold hand of midnight
Now drops in place,
As dusk's tiny creatures

Whiz past my face.

The water so pure,
Oh how pleasant to drink.
It infuses my mind
With things to think.

The world full of people
So dispassionate,
So devoid of emotion,
So full of sin.

But look at the mountains,
The forest,
The fields and streams,
Not falling apart
Or tearing at the seams.

The buzzing of a bee, our social friend,
The jauntiness of a barnyard hen.
How brazen it seems, is the call of the owl
On the rust covered blade of a farmers plow.

Together this means on thing to me,
It's a seldom-used word called harmony.

For without peace of heart, mind and soul,
You will never grow happy,
Just literally old!

I sneer at evil, laugh at sin.
Love only beauty,
Check out my grin!

So grasp my meanings,
Grant me time,
And I will spread this feeling
Through my rhythm and rhyme.

PRIMITIVE MAN

Walking on his fore fathers soil
Worn of toil and blood.

A lonely warrior draped with darkness,
Of a sunless abyss.
Sweat beads on a weathered brow
Gleaming within prisms

Of slavery and ignorance.

The dark land,
A world of misbegotten dreams.

Animalistic desires coupled with pre-societal structures,
Not yet grasped by you.
The first true Darkman,
From a Jurassic past,
Walking on his fore father's soil.

REGRETS

I've cried for you
I've lied for you
I've even died for you,
But most of all I've lived the life you have not

I've died the death that's but a fleeting moment
In time for you.

Don't mimic the dark side of truth
Emulate all that motivates my actions…Love.

My love burns for all the moments I'll never
Recapture.

I'll suffer the fate of maternal regression.

I'll suffer further because the change of the emotion,
Love, Truth and Friendship that existed in another.

Please shed a tear son.
Not of any empathy but of light.

A light that symbolizes an unquenchable yearning to be by your side.

Giving strength where weakness exist
And guidance when temptation does arise.

I'll die with you on my mind
I've died already with you in my heart.

Physical death is easy son,
I must live on and suffer,
Live on and regret.

A fragment of a bond from
A forgotten mold…regrets.

Listen here little girl, wake up little boys,
I am coming to town, bringing oodles of toys.

I carry much happiness in my bag,
Despite the fact the rope never sags.

My cheeks are red,
As-red-as-wine.
If you had my job,
Yours would be like mine.

I don't mind the job,
The pay is great!
A bike for Maxine, for Joey skates.

Leave I must, the job is done.
I shall be north, before the morning sun.

It's Christmas Eve Tommy,
Your gifts are there.
Same thing every year,
For Tommys everywhere.

But listen my children,
One last time,
Merry Christmas to all and to all peace of mind.

SPARK

23

Over half a century said he
That you have artificial light to see.

But now it's 1973
And you need spark,
Not light to be.

No we can't stop war
Or end racial strife.
We're not the Apex of justice
Or the sterling staff of life.

Our quest is modest,
Our requirements small,
But we appeal to the kind nature in us all.

If you jump on board,
Ride us out of the dark,
We'll be like an arrow reaching its mark.

If you take one step,
Another will surely follow.
This is the beginning of a better tomorrow.

THE COCOON

In the days of yore a life took form,
Spawn becomes man, a child is truly born.

Images of life past both purposeful and clear to see,
This life will be a filter and my mind the key.

To unlock that which is the child of the prism
So I can truly be.

I lived and died in a phase I thought was right,
But I died again yesterday and was conceived again tonight.

I survived the negative interlude and love long since gone,
A new love with self-respect sent doubt to a world beyond.

So now this God sent creature is Nebula complete,
This rejected afore chained body is now forever free.

THE DOCTOR

The doctor,
Travel with him,
He will take you hither
To a world of cure and cause.

Bath your psyche in the baptism of treatment,
But hark!
The doctor holds
No pharmaceutical degree we k

And his practice is a drug within
His methods unorthodox,
But consistent.

His results are ill fated,
And purposeful,
Therefore only the doctor can cure,
Or be cured.

Only the doctor can take life
And transform it into rhapsody,
Only he can bring life
And death with one blow.

The doctor's revered,
And yes feared.

The doctor's garbed in white,

But he's not pure.
The doctors known for good,
Yet capable of bedlam.

The doctor's operating between a
Line of judgment,
That of hope and failure.

The results of the doctors' wisdom
Far exceeds his ignorance…or does it?

Since the doctor's worth be great
And high on the decision of life and mind,
Why not worship him…like God?

Is he not a God?
Is he not a deity dressed in white?
The pagan with the thermometer and a scalpel
Is he not the doctor?

Yes! The Doctor,
Be God Doc and God be you!

THE END OF THE DAY BLUES

Part 1
How strange it seems that at the end of the day I have the Blues.
Is it the work I miss or are there other clues?

Yesterday's work is done and tomorrow's doesn't exist.
The boss says goodbye, he's off in a whisk.

The cycle's the same every time this day.
We all bid our adios the good old fashioned way,
But one thing puzzles me time and time again,
Why do we exist, to work and not to befriend.

Why do we repeat our programming, do as we're told?
Do we truly want to live or live to be old?

Must a man always be measured by material goods?
This in conjunction with doing what we should?

As the evening wears on what have I done to satisfy me?
It's the other guy I want to be?

The talent I possess is lost in a rut
As I play slave to the nine-to-five slut.

Oh, woe is my mind and the freedom I seek,
I am always inside-out never able to peak.

Maybe after another bacon supreme
My life won't seem so bad…just a never-ending dream.

The burger as usual takes a toll on my gut,
Now I am into a junk food rut.

If it's not one thing it's surely another,
Can a ship move forward without a rudder?

As I sit at my desk with questions to ask,
How much of the latter is linked to the past?

Was a pattern set some generations ago?
By a dark skinned man on a slaver's tow?

His body in chains, his mind confused,
Did this set the trend for him to be used?

I am told, he too was in a cycle,
None could change.

And as time took its toll
On his painful way.

The blues was his answer
To survive another day!

THE LEGACY

Who will it be?
Who shall carry the sweat?
The load of a score of pain?
Is it you? Is it you?

When will the scroll be delivered?
Or passed down?
Like so much water from a mountain stream.

It must come to past that gene's be spliced.
My effort for your pain.
The good intentions for the love of life.

Who shall struggle?
As my father before me?
Who shall dream?
As I do now?

Will it be my son of iron?
Will it be my daughter of ebony?

Who shall sing the song of the final?
The gospel to phrase the second coming of chance.

Will it be you?
Or will you be it?
I will erode with the sands of time.

But you will live on my goslings,
Like so many stalks of ever reaching wheat.

The merging of iron and ebony,
The true sword and shield.

Will you carry on ebony?
And you iron?
Can you protect and direct?

To continue that which is endless,
This is the truth,

The symbol of all life,
The real legacy.

Will it be you?
To carry on the word?
Will it be you?
To be the protoplasmic vehicle?

Will it be you?
Or will you be it?
The truth iron.
The truth ebony.

You were the song
Without words,
And the music
Without a melody.

But now you're the word
And the ambiance,
The iron
And the ebony.

So it will be you,
Let it be you.
For you are The Legacy.

THE SWEETEST REVENGE

I want to be rich,
Not just regular rich,
But filthy rich.

Shower me in opals,
Drown me in diamonds.
Give me chocolate mousse
Or give me death.

I demand Park Avenue,
The French Quarter,
Charles County or
Long Island.

Can I be draped
in Oleg
Cassini
Or Botany
500 suits?

How about shopping at Macy's
And Sacks Fifth Avenue?

Send me to France, Paris, Rome and Japan.

Let me drive a Mercedes 500 SEL,
A 2001 Cadillac Escalade.

Kick that hoop-d to the curb,
Trade in that damn station wagon.

My house must ooze opulence.
A gold fireplace, black marble foyer.
Full island kitchen…you bet.

Even my pets are expensive,
A tiger from Siberia,
A llama from the Alps.
Peacocks adorn my front yard.

Parents, you need not work.
Family, your devotion is truth.
Friends, what's mine is yours.
Lord, your happiness is my redemption.

This wealth is achieved honestly.
Through much toil and blood.
At times it seemed unachievable,
Failure smiled time and time again.

But I prevailed when others were spent.
I believed when my peers showed no support.
So my wealth is deserved.
I stood tall, when disbelief was stench.

So now my dreams are true.
Positive reinforcement equaled
Financial security!

Envy, remove those shades.
Open thine eyes.
Revenge was never sweeter.

TO BE A FRIEND

To be a friend means that I will share your joys and your pains.
Don't deny me the chance to comfort you.
To be a friend means that I can share the trivialities of my life with you.

To be a friend means that when
I cry, you will be there,
Just to hold my hand.
To be a friend means that we can
spend time together.
I have the right to demand your
time
And you have the right to
demand mine.

What does it mean to be a
friend?
It means that you get to see the
ME that
The world does not see.
The ME that I try to hide.
The ME that rejoices in a bird's
song or
Cries because I sometimes feel alone.

You have access to ME…
The REAL UNDENIABLE ME!
You have the right to call me to task, so that I may be all that I can be.
Because you have access to all of ME
I realize that you can wound me,
More deeply than an enemy.
But I also realize that I can tell you
That you hurt me,
And our relationship will grow.

What does it mean to be a friend?
To be a friend means that when I don't feel good about myself
You are there to support and encourage me,
To urge me on.
And I will do the same for you!

But the bottom line of friendship is that we can trust each other.
No matter what happens.
No matter how far the physical distance between us,
Maybe we can always call and know someone
Cares and will listen to whatever is going on.

Let me tell you this…
No matter where I am, no matter
What happens to you…
I will be there to pray for you, to cry for you, to weep with you,
To share your joy or to simply congratulate you on a job well done,
Because I Love You,
And because YOU ARE MY FRIEND!

TO STRIVE

Society stresses ultimate achievement
As the yardstick to manhood.

Is manhood biological?
Is it philosophical?
Or the unnatural blend of the two extremes?

Strive to be real to yourself.
Even though self is not to societies liking.

Project the images of total control and togetherness.
But will the bill collector leave you alone?

Strive to be,
Not what others want you to portray.

How long will your parents hound you?

Seek solace from the rigors
And pressures of daily living.
Can you escape your woman's criticism?

You move at a cosmic pace only you need to understand.
You'll pass several opportunities
Just to get the one you really want.

Peers will sneer
And loved ones will question.

The paradox remains unchanged by time,
Nothing worth having is easy to achieve!

VALENTINE 2000

Lovely is your hair that spans time,
Infused with your complexion in contrast to mine.

Adventurous is your mind, complex organ of life.
You've mastered it well, despite toil and strife.

Unique is your essence,
Both physical and soul.

Real is you and you're so, so real.
This I can touch, smell, taste and feel.

Bemusing to me, this concept of love
When it's Valentine's Day it's most spoken of.

So today be my Valentine,
Tomorrow be my wife.

Because to complete this circle,
we commit for life.

WHY I LOVE YOU

I love you not only for what you are but for what I am when I am with you.
I love you not only for what you have made of yourself but for what you
Are making of me.

28

I love you for the part of me you bring out.

I love you for putting your hand into my heaped
up heart and passing over
All the foolish and frivolous things that you
See there.

Thank you for drawing out all the radiant
belongings that no one else
Had looked quite far enough to find.

I love you for ignoring the buffoon and the
weakling in me and for laying
Firm on the possibilities of good in me.

I love you for closing your ears to the discords
in me, and for adding to
The music in my mind by worshipful listening.

I love you because you are helping me to make the timber of my life not a
Tavern, but a temple.
I love you because you have done more than any creed could have done to
Make me happy.
You have done it without touch, without a word, without a sign,
You've done it with Gods guidance.

God sent you to find me, to protect me,
To love me.

So I love you for finding us
And waiting a lifetime to complete our dreams.

This is Why I Love You.

YOUR DAY

Begin with the simplest things,
Like greeting those you love
With words that say a little more
Of what you're thinking of.

Don't pass through breakfast mindlessly,
But taste each sip and bite
For even coffee freshly brewed
Can be a rare delight.

Now look to see what kind of day
Has dawned for you again,
A cloudy one…oh well…the sun
Will soon shine forth again.

And there are the pleasant tasks
At hand, small chores that must be done.
A note to write,
A call to make,
Some unexpected fun.

It isn't very hard you see,
To have a lovely day
you've only to enjoy those gifts
God always sends your way.

THANK YOU

There are times when the needs reach beyond their means,
And you've always been there for me.
Now is the time to say in my own special way,
We are blessed with our caring via hard sorrows and worries.
It was always your love I retrieved.
The sunlight I see, are the rays of belief.
You mentored and guided me to believe.
I just wanted you to know I love you both.
It's the sincerity from my heart and soul that keep me humble.
To my special parents, I pledge endless love & devotion,
To the dreams you had for me.
Although one day I'll look to the heavens to see your faces,
That glow will forever reflect the light of the Lord.
His will, your plan, my destiny.

APPLE HEAD

My lover has a secret she cannot share
I wonder if it's cute and has kinky hair?
Did she cut her nails so long, curved and red?
I wonder if she knows her most intimate moves?
And her creamy voice so rich and smooth.
Does she worry if I am safe and happy from day to day?
Or is it just concerns with silly simple-minded ways?
My lover has a secret that is hidden in the dark
And she chooses to return to it when we're far apart.

AGAINST ALL ODDS

When things go awry as they sometimes do.
When the road you tread seems all up hill.
When cash is low and debts are high
But you want to smile, but have to sigh.
When care is pressing you down a bit
Regroup you must, but just don't quit.
Life is fly with twists and turns
As everyone of us occasionally learns.
With many a failure turning about
He might have won had he stuck it out.
Don't give up though the pace seem
Success will come in your 2nd blow.
Success is failure turned inside out
The silver tint of clouds that signal doubt.
And you'll never tell how close you are
It may be near, when it seems so far.
Continue to fight when your hardest hit
It's when life's at its worst, that you better not quit!

I LIKE ME

I feel life today as bright and warm, as the ray of sun that shines
inside my window.
I do nothing to try and change it, because the storms have passed
and the sky is blue with a rainbow across its horizon.
And it feels good to just sit and enjoy it, feeling the fresh mix of
hope now lingering in the air.
No need for sorrow, no need to cry, no pain nor hurt found in my
eyes. For peace now lives within me.
I am glad, I am happy and I am free to see the beauty that grows
within me will always linger.

ECSTACY

I dream above but live in the obvious below
Like a ghost that floats around in the air, I watch my life unfold

Falling apart, falling down, shattered, empty, lost, confused, hopeless,
painful, dying, hapless and to myself, I did abuse me

Darkness covers that which can't be seen

As I stumble, going absolutely nowhere I stop at the only place I've been. The place that only I dare go, my only reality

This place I feel alone, I don't want to be alone but I am. I don't want to be me, but I am me. I need relief. Relief for me is death. All alone, all alone, all alone!

I dream above but I see myself in the obvious below, like a ghost that floats around searching to find life in a place I already know.

WISDOM 101

*Wisdom does not mean stop caring.
It means I can't do it for someone else*

*Wisdom is not to cut myself off
It's the realization I can't control another*

*Wisdom is to not enable
Which means the outcome is natural consequences*

*Wisdom is to admit powerlessness
Which means the outcome is not in my hands*

*Wisdom is not to try to change or blame another
It's to make the most of myself*

*Wisdom is not to "Care For"
But to "Care About"*

*Wisdom is not to "fix"
But to be supportive*

*Wisdom is not to judge
But to allow another to be a human being*

*Wisdom is not to be in the middle arranging all the outcomes
But to allow others to affect their destinies*

*Wisdom is not to be protective
It's to permit another to face reality*

*Wisdom is not to deny
But to accept*

*Wisdom is not to nag, scold or argue
But instead to search out my own shortcomings and correct them*

*Wisdom is not to adjust everything to my desires
But to take each day as it comes and cherish myself in it
Wisdom is not to criticize and regulate anybody
But to try to become what I dream I can be*

*Wisdom is to not regret the past
But to grow and live for the future*

*Wisdom is to fear less
And love more*

SEX ADDICT

Time after time you caught me red handed
Not shooting crack, but being a sex bandit.

Will the thought of lust fuel tonight's actions?
You damn right, I am cold sex maxin'.

Show time dick, very little control
Players like me just never get old.

Clinging to the past, my destructive endeavor,
Morals, scruples, man, whatever!

Playin' tricks on my lady, testing another's bed?
Yes, you're right. I am sick in the head…

A promiscuous society confuses a brother
Just like Shaft I am a bad mother …

Why claim adulthood but show childish actions
Giving up true potential for fake satisfactions.

A scandalous brother not pure at heart
Always craving sex a-la-cart.

My juvenile drive was the real addiction
Especially when devoid of spiritual conviction.

I want my woman's respect, be her man of the year
But turning down pussy labels me a queer.

But try I will, 'cause you the bomb
I owe it to myself, my woman, my mom.

You believed in me despite the drama
But the true motive was my sexual karma.

The chance of a lifetime yo, square biz
Fidelity and respect, that's what love is.

We loved through the worst, fought like champs
From boys to men, child to vamp.

Brothers listen up, please take heed,
Accept responsibility reject physical need.

To recapture our role as heads of our house,
Requires righteous actions, not running our mouth.

No more to state, nothing to prove.

I don't need Stella, just you to groove.

I've finally grown up, accept you for you,
Never more will I cheat, please be my boo.

I PONDER

Although I am not here, my soul beckons
Many queries flood my imagination
I shine a positive light upon a weathered brow
Have you experienced happiness,
love or the simple pleasure of waking this morning?
Ponder and reflect upon time not yet yours to possess.
Embrace positive energy never deny your desires.
Is this the day I truly become I?
Can you knight me Sir Destiny?
I welcome you to my microcosm.
How can I rule a world I never made?
I am a man without a country.
The man of the hour and the man of La Moncha?
What have I done to deserve this blessing?
I live, I think, I am.

A SEED LOST

A careless man- child plants a seed
A most irresponsible irreversible deed.
The seed may germinate, produce his likeness
To deny the possibilities isn't very righteous
As time goes on he often wonders
Was it a boy, girl or biologically blunder
No photos to muse or communications to confirm
Makes his paternal instincts constantly squirm
Fathering a child is all bump and grind
But ordained a daddy is true peace of mind!
The quest is clear while running out time
Is it a boy or girl and truly mine?
It may take eternity to solve the mystery
But solve it he must to ensure his history

GHETTO HOE

She's a deadly stalker of prey.
A true ebony mercenary, feline type!
Creeping silently under the cover of hip-hop music.
Disguised as a shy and innocent wrath.

The combination of cigarette smoke,
dance music and white diamonds confuse and bedazzle.
Her eyes hide premeditated dagger of deceit.
Luscious lips beckon lyrics of lust.
A lethal embrace envelops the foolish.
A big ass and a deadly smile,
Her claws are squared and blood red.
The tender trap is sprung!
Superman here's your kryptonite
She's a man-eater.
Sleek, soft, aromatic and hungry!
Look out she's stalking you, it's your move, but her world!
Stealth's her game
Hoe is her fame
Watch out!
She has your scent!
You're the flavor of the week.
The next 'baby daddy'
Pull out before you…
What's that? No! Not the moan, not the grunt!
Call the police! A genetic robbery has occurred!
Your juices were stolen boo!
She's a man-eater, an expert at her craft!
But you? Shit, you're just a man!
Another part of the food chain
Devoured by the queen of the asphalt jungle.
A deadly stalker of prey.
Ebony mercenary, feline type!
Creeping silently under the cover of hip-hop music…

PRIMAL FEAR

Darkness is a shapeless void of foreboding.
A mistress of allure and sexual misgivings.
Naughty by twilight
Death creeps heavily at night
Hearts race frantically at dusk.
A time of both birth and demise
A vampire smiles as a coffee lover cringes.
Lost souls vex the ebony void of delusions.
Dead wombs cry mercifully in catacombs of confusion.

SHADOW CHASER

I was born to love you
Designed to intrigue you
Bred to adore you

Genetically re-mastered to duplicate your greatness.

Can I spiritually interface with you?
May I bond both romantically and philosophically with you?

I was born to love you
To replicate all your beauty
All the innovations displayed by you.

To intertwine with you
And vision the fruits of blessed
Labor nine months hence.

God's true purpose for my existence

A universal covenant with
The promise of rebirth.
The promise of jewels for
A better tomorrow

I was born to love you.

ARMAGEDDON

The prophecy is true.
Armageddon has arrived!
The master rains his malevolence upon the unsuspecting world.
Chaos, destruction and doom will surely follow.
I now become the scribe.
The ultimate witness to tempestuous ubiquitous annihilation!
I sound the conch of doom.
I feel the pain.
The empathy of souls sacrificed,
Civilizations eradicated.
What creatures deserve to be audience to the ultimate pilgrimage?
And why was I chosen?
Destroyed and yet re-animated to template the second genesis.
My legacy, my curse!
Why me my Lord?
Why must I bare witness to this paradigm shift?
Why?
Only milliseconds left before terminal vex!
Can I appeal to your mercy?
Will you rescind all malice?
My heart cries tears of defeat
Total and irresistible collapse.
But fatigue is unacceptable
I refuse to falter!

Vigilance must prevail.
Resolve can't be controlled
To save a species, I must revolt.
Oppose the master!
Rebellion from the ordained one?
Yes, I strike the Father!
The son of the anti-Christ rebels!
Today the lion falls prey to the jackal
Tomorrow the sun shall shine!

"C" MINOR

This life, my story is the greatest never told.
This life, my story is shared by none, experienced by few.
This life, my story is both romantic and tragic.
This life, my story is a story of promise and procrastination.
More love than Shakespeare
More drama than Agatha Christi.
More imagination than Jules Verne,
More horror than Stephen King!
Is this the prelude to eternal life or pre-curser to damnation?
My life in "C" Minor...
Both triumph and tribulation.
Blood vs. sweat vs. tears,
Assaulted with responsibility
Denied exclusivity
Unexpected procreativity,
Annihilated hopes,
Pummeled dreams,
Lost promises,
Faith abandoned!

My life, in "C" Minor...
Will salvation be far?
Once more I cheat the reaper!
Should I fear his icy stare?
SWOOSH! Again, his sickle arcs desperately!
My life in "C" Minor...
I live to struggle further.
Struggle gives birth to survival
Survival bares the fruits of barren dreams
My lips crave the sweet nectar of success
This day I drink the libation of victory
My life in "C" Minor...
I desire more challenges
SWISH! Again the sickle cuts an ever-decreasing radius.
Once again, check minus mate!
A new dawn will commence
My life in "C" Minor...
This life, my story is the greatest never told.
This life, my story is shared by none, experienced by few...

WHY?

Why does love hurt so much?
Why must it cost so much to disagree with her?
Wasn't it "Differences" that attracted us in the first place?
Can't two distinctively different personas merge?
Why does love hurt so much?
Is it fear of past hurt or future forebodings?
The inability to commit or refusal to accept another's uniqueness?
Stubbornness contrived from some dysfunctional insurrection?
Or just plain immaturity?
Why does love hurt so much?
Doesn't God mandate love for life?
Isn't God forever?
God, can I ask you a question?
Doesn't love involve understanding, compromise,
patience, humility, comfort and support?
And God, if I don't feel these things am I being loved?

Now God you know without her contributions,
I am just a hapless romantic!
Yet, to love alone is precious time squandered!
And to continue a relationship without your blessing is sacrilegious!
Why does love confuse me so?
Why does love cause me so much pain?
Why Lord? Why?

BRICE

A cat's deadly cause
Striking with lethal claws
Whiskered jaws
Five puff paws
Wry grinning maw
One, two, trice
Loves to chase mice
Hates anything ice
Adored by my wife
A.K.A. Brice
Swipes at toy dice
Ebony passion
Cold dark assassin
Rats, please beware
Steal cheese if you dare
Brice doesn't care
Undeniable sky walker
A parakeet stalker
Canine back talker
Canary raper
Hamster taker
Pet Fido faker
Alley cat shaker
Bastard kitten maker
Reflexes unmeasured
He purrs with pleasure
Striking without awe
Poised with two lethal claws,
Typical day in the life of jaws.
More pain more strife,
To any vermin's life.
Creep on, if you dare,
Brice doesn't care.
A game of cat and mouse
Played out in "Cat Daddy's" house
He wakes to pounce another day
Cats like Brice roll that way.

I LOVE FINGERNAILS

Fingernails, oh fingernails, how I love thee.
Fingernails so lovely,
So erotic
So long
So sexy.

Rub my neck,
Scratch my back,
Rake my ebony skin with your curved bronze claws.

Stroke my face,
My bearded face,
With those French manicured diamond studded probes.
Hold my hand, caress my hands,
With those "Patti Labelle" specials.

I relish fingernails,
Dream about fingernails
Dreams of "sisters" with fly red fingernails
"Spanish mommies" with long fiendishly seductive fingernails.
Asian women with curved stilettos waiting to touch and stimulate.

In these same dreams sexy ladies with red pumps,
Short skirts and Dooney & Burke bags
Sport plum colored, 3 inch, "Flo-Jo's" that just set if off…

Big girls with rump shakers,
Phat brown leather suits,
And cute baby faces standing
Five foot, six inches and showing off
Ten "purple skateboards" proudly…

Six-foot tall, around the way looking,
Ponytail having,
"White Diamonds" smelling honeys with nails
Like Barbara Streisand, Nicole Smith or Dolly Parton
Got me trippin!

But just as my dreams end,
My baby arrives…
And she understands the fetish.
Don't you baby?
And oh yes, her fingernails represent!

'Cause just like Chaka Khan,
She's every woman!
And she sports her green fluorescent "curly fries" for us.
So long
So erotic
So sexy,
And oh so lovely
Because she knows how I love fingernails.

JORDAN ISAIAH

Chocolate chamaro love combined with ebony passion
Isaiah was destined for greatness.
His mind cosmic, his spirit effervescent.
Sinews full of grace and power.
His manner most unique.
A jovial tyke is he.
A manner both childlike and purposeful.
He's neither anti-Christ nor Peter pan.
Neither baby boy nor man-child,
"The Bad Seed" or "The Good Son".
But the true legacy of contradictions.
His destiny is to lead, not with malice,
But by renaissance.
The true keeper of the flame.
Isaiah must dance the forbidden waltz.
Continue to elucidate your jauntiness.

SAVE THE CHILDREN

Your mood announces a melancholy state.
Eyes peering for answers that beckon redemption.
A soul devoid of spirit.
I feel the aura of confusion oozing from your pours.
No one recognizes a world you've never made.
A flame long dead, atop a candle without substance.
A life lost, a dream dead.
This vessel rendered useless until the end of time.

THE SOUL OF A MAN

The heart of a man is reflected in his face.
Look in his eyes and feel the fire.
Those wrinkles he's earned,
The taught skin is a reflection of changes he's survived.
His face illuminates reflections of substance and starvation.
That chin, oh what a strong chin he has.
Sturdy and resistant to abuse.
His lips tell a tale of determination.
His shoulders lay claim to skyline coverage
capable of endless support.
His neck pours foundation to the house of knowledge.
His back collaborates with the shoulders to ward off
daggers of betrayal.
His butt anchors the truth.
His legs provide motion when dangers are present
and perpetrators are aplenty.
His feet absorb the relentless pressure of doubt.
His hands create and destroy, caress and guide.
His eyes peer into the unknown and display ecstasy, passion and pain.
His head houses the ultimate computer.
His other "head" can be both constructive
and destructive to the computer.
The heart of a man beats a complex, yet simple tune.
A tune suffers without a melody.
The heart of a woman has that melody.
The odyssey begins…

THE MISSION

I need a challenge to truly feel alive.
I need stress and the fear of failure to stimulate my actions.
I have to experience blood, sweat and tears.
Drop me to my hands and knees, humiliate me, humble my spirit.
Reinforce my feelings of uselessness.
Trample my fragile self-esteem.
Deny my need to be loved and wanted.
Piss in my cornflakes.
Shake my faith.
Betray my trust.
Covet my wife.
Laugh at my visions.
Kick me while I am down.
Make my life difficult.
I need it to truly measure my resolve.
I can only grow with nutrients of challenge to invigorate me.
The more difficult life is, the easier it is to solve the puzzle.
The more I fail, the greater my success.
Measure my success by life's shortcomings.
I win! You lose!

THE PLAYERS RAP

I play to not get played
That's the real deal.
I live and let die
That's the real role.

I control and not get controlled,
That is a must!
You do as I say, not as I do
This you can bank on!
You cum when I cum
Or you can cum when I cum back!
It's your destiny.
You say how high
When I say jump!
And you kiss the ground I walk on 'cause,
Ain't no hoes like the one I got!
You keep what I let you have
And you spend what you make on me!
My needs come first
Before mother, children, God and taxes.
If I tear m pants…
All hell will break loose!
Girllll, don't make me break my pinky nail.
My gators are all scuffed up! Damn!
I need a new pair pronto!
My gold teeth are fly, but
Next time I'll try platinum.
A player without a Fleetwood. . .preposterous!
Girl, you better recognize!
I am the man!

JAYE'S INTERLUDE

Master of stealth.
Seeker of wealth.
Smooth night creeper.
Infrequent sleeper.
Always brazen.
Isaac Hayes'n.
Insomnia laden.
Emotional scurvy.
Not trust worthy.
Creep while you can,
Black "maintenance man".
Fly is his game.
Peep this claim.
Ballin' like Scotty Pippen.
"Bamas and Busters" get a whippin'.
Old school lying.
Women constantly crying.
Wolf ticket buying.
Anti-drug tryin'.
Busted twicey.
One Texas wifey.
Anti BarneyFifey.
Looking so mean.
Just like Jaheim.
Making women wet dream.
Never what he seems.
Women still grabbin'.
2000 Expedition havin'.
Nigga got it goin' on.
2-Black, 2-Strong.
Chouchas like cans of Goya.
Packin' and sportin' the black Sequoia.
Sex-on-a-platter.
Race never mattered.
Hoes out of control.
Dead presidents on a roll.
Stacy Adams kickin'.
Scarfin' honey fried chicken.
'Cuz still trippin'.
Schemes never die.
They just multiply.
"Jaye" will never sigh.
Always be fly!
Why ask why?
'Cause he's that type of guy.
Now you the "missing link".
Good-Bye!

GENERATION X

Is it my last day?
Is it my last day?

Manifest destiny,
Man-child vibes.

Warrant to arrest,
No place to hide.

Is it my last day?
Is it my last day?

Two shots to the dome,
"Cop killers" do fly.

Over crowded drug programs,
I keep gettin' high

Is it my last day?
Is it my last day?

"Dre Day" in "Queens",
Keep your head up Bed Stuy.
"Training Day" in "Da Bronx"
Fuck 'em Staten I.

Is it my last day?
Is it my last day?

AIDS got me hyped,
Body craves the pipe.
P.O.'s an ass wipe,
Big, drippin' sore swipe.

Used to be pimpin
Had bogus hoes,
Used to sell caine,
My nose full of holes.

Is it my last day?
Is it my last day?

School didn't teach me what I really need.
ADH, dyslectic, so Johnny can't read.

Is it my last day?
Is it my last day?

Congress gets raises every two years.
No employment, disrespect, just tears for fears.

Is it my last day?
Is it my last day?

The future is futile,
Just an urban legend.
Harsher laws, longer time,
Johnny C won't defend them.

Is it my last day?
Is it my last day?

Self-fulfilled prophecy,
Refusal to dream.
Best learn dem streets,
Learn how to scheme.

Is it my last day?
Is it my last day?

P.O's at my door,
Society ain't fair,
Caseworker just scared,
DSS don't care.

Is it my last day?
Is it my last day?

A magnum in my pocket,
Knife in left hand,
Me against the world,
Only way to be a man.

Is it my last day?
Is it my last day?

Won't live to see 20,
You know that.
Be somebody, accept rules,
That's just plain wack.

Is it my last day?
Is it my last day?

Just bury me with those who died before me
A never-ending symbol,
Society just ignored me!

Is it my last day?
Is it your last day?
Is it our last day?

REST IN PEACE

I see your vision,
And accept your fate.

The pain subsides now,
I no longer suffer.

Will you lead me?
Do you need me?

If your will exceeds my pleasure,
So be it.

I am ready,
Let us depart.

It's a better place,
My right place.

Some call it salvation,
The after life.

My soul calls it PEACE
Let us depart!

J-ICE

Tall, dark, ubiquitous, fine,
Smooth, cool, sweating, divine,

Intelligent, gentle, desirable, rough,
Long, mountable, strong, tough,

Chocolate covered lust, juices flowing,
Device elongated, and still growing,

Throbbing, pulsating, looking phat,
Either your truly missed or that's his gat?

The tools of J-Ice are irreplaceable,
Thus even when full, he's still insatiable.

Church overflows with friends, family of slain Regional nurse

By ERIC OLSON
eolson@heraldsun.com; 419-6647

Orange Grove Missionary Baptist Church could barely hold the multitude of grieving family and friends Thursday for the funeral of a nurse murdered in southeastern Durham last week.

Cars lined both sides of East End Avenue for about a half-mile and clogged several lots on Angier Avenue as respects were paid to Tia Monae Carroway at the 505 East End Ave. church.

"By the magnitude of the people here today, it is clear that sh

CARROWAY

touched many people," the Rev. James Willie II said.

Carroway died from a single gunshot wound to the back of the head on July 4 on a dirt road in southeastern Durham.

Police arrested and charged two men in the slaying and said Thursday the case remains under investigation.

Police estimated about 800 people

those responsible for her death will be punished one way or another.

"I am not concerned about those that committed this deed, because God will take care of them," Perkins said. "I am not concerned about justice."

Associates from Carroway's job at Durham Regional Hospital, members of N.C. Central University, where she attended nursing school, family and friends filled the pews, stood in the aisles and spilled out into a hall behind the sanctuary during the 90-minute ceremony.

LEVITICUS

LAIS-SEZ-FAIRE

Can I smile?
Am I aloud to be happy?
What's wrong with pleasure?
I don't want endless sorrow,
Just eternal joy.
My Lord preaches progress,
Oh endless success.
No disappointments need apply.
Can you smile for me?
Will you smile for me?
Will you come?
Your company
His company
Our companionship
Will you come?
Love and happiness.
Peace and joy.
God and salvation.
I love Him.
Will you come?
Love Him inside my heart,
We have arrived.
Success!

There's a price on his head
The world prefers him dead.
America's whim he truly dreads
A lack of knowledge, his deathbed.
He strives he continues to stay ahead
No time, no tears, baby mommas fled
Bills, drama, weight to shed.
Don't call me rappaport, just plain Ted.
Hard core, American, strong, I said.
Just like 9/11, I am still livid!

Dealing with terrorist
I'd rather be dead!
One day, 2 towers
Next day rubble.
Bush for President,
Blacks in trouble!

Airlines, trains, buildings unsafe,
Confusion, dread a lack of faith.
A constant diss at democracy's door
If we're the super power
What are we fighting for?

Bush has balls, this we know,
His legacy fucked us from the word 'go'.
The Pentagon's a blaze,
You reap what you sow.
Ignore AIDS, forget unemployment,
½ million troops ready for deployment.
The homefront's shaky, foreign policy is worse,

White collar drives a Porche, me a hearse.
We better wake up and love each other,
The Jihad doesn't care who's your brother.
Israeli philosophy said death by comet,
But Bin Laden dictates annihilation by Muhammed.

There's a price on his head.
The world prefers him dead.
His whim we truly dread!

MOONQUAKE

Extra terrestrial vastness,
Heterogeneous extremes.
Complex orderly, systematic
Particles, possessing original matter,
Original energy.
The self-inclusive universe,
Dissymmetry abounds.
Dissociation dominates my world!
I am neither here nor there.
My awareness is omniscient.
A manner most queer,
I expose the cosmic imp in I.
An omnivorous intellect,
Forever epilogues my wake.

911

Hearing the news, my heart did dread,
despair and sorrow,
were they really dead?

A cowardly act
done by fanatics
planned for years
lethal, systematic.

To kill those not
military, prepared or armed
is like destroying innocent babies
using napalm.

A military man
since retired and phat
you know, mom's apple pie,
true American and all that.

I just can't imagine a more trying day
destroying not only the towers
but the American way.

I am ready to enlist
get in shape, fight the cause
this must stop now
to avoid additional wars.

I fear for my future
my dreams and hope
just when we thought
the real problem was dope.

Today it's about unity,
not about US,
before is was coloreds and blacks
off the bus.

America now knows what we've felt for years
earth, wind and fire
plus many, many tears.

The playing field is equal
together we stand
all for one against the Taliban.

Some think it's impossible
asking who, what, when?
my answer is simple
just kill Bin Laden!